GW00720399

SAMSON: LOSER OR WINNER?

Samson: Loser or Winner? by Hugo Bouter
Cover design by Boland BNO Visual Forces
Copyright © 2001 Chapter Two, London

All rights reserved. No part of this publication may be reproduced or transmitted in any form or by any means, electronic or mechanical, including photocopying, recording, or storage in any information retrieval system, without written permission from Chapter Two.

ISBN 1 85307 174 9
Printed in the Netherlands
Bible quotations are from the New King James Version

Distributors:

- Bible, Book and Tract Depot, 23 Santa Rosa Avenue, Ryde, NSW 2112, Australia
- Bible House, Gateway Mall, 35 Tudor Street, Bridgetown, Barbados, WI
- Believers Bookshelf, 5205 Regional Road 81, Unit 3, Beamsville, ON, L0R 1B3, Canada
- Bible Treasury Bookstore Inc., 46 Queen Street, Dartmouth, NS, B2Y 1G1, Canada
- El-Ekhwa Library, 3 Anga Hanem Street, Shoubra, Cairo, Egypt
- Bibles & Publications Chrétiennes, 30 Rue Châteauvert, 26000 Valence, France
- CSV, An der Schloßfabrik 30, 42499 Hückeswagen, Germany
- Christian Truth Bookroom, Paddisonpet, Tenali 522 201, Andhra Pradesh, India
- Words of Life Trust, 3 Chuim, Khar, Mumbai 400 052, India
- Uit het Woord der Waarheid, Postbox 260, 7120 AG Aalten, Netherlands
- Bible and Book Depot, Box 25119, Christchurch 5, New Zealand
- Echoes of Truth, No 11 Post Office Road, P.O. Box 2637, Mushin, Lagos, Nigeria
- Kristen Litteratur, Elvebakkveien 9, 4270 Åkrehamn, Norway
- Grace & Truth Book-room, 87 Chausee Road, Castries, St. Lucia, WI
- Beröa Verlag, Zellerstraße 61, 8038 Zürich, Switzerland
- Éditions Bibles et Littérature Chrétienne, 4 Rue du Nord, CH 1800 Vevey, Switzerland
- Chapter Two Bookshop, 199 Plumstead Common Road, London, SE18 2UJ, UK
- HoldFast Bible & Tract Depot, 100 Camden Road, Tunbridge Wells, Kent, TN1 2QP, UK
- Words of Truth, P.O. Box 147, Belfast, BT8 4TT, Northern Ireland, UK
- Believers Bookshelf Inc., Box 261, Sunbury, PA 17801, USA

HUGO BOUTER

SAMSON: LOSER OR WINNER?

Samson as a type of Christ

Chapter Two - London

*"And the Angel of the L*ORD *said to him,*
'Why do you ask My name, seeing it is wonderful?' "

Judges 13:18

" 'And she will bring forth a Son, and you shall call
*His name J*ESUS, *for He will save His people from their sins'.*
Now all this was done that it might be fulfilled which was spoken
by the Lord through the prophet, saying: 'Behold, a virgin shall be
with child, and bear a Son, and they shall call His name Immanuel',
which is translated, 'God with us' ."

Matthew 1:21-23

CONTENTS

INTRODUCTION 7

1. HE SHALL BEGIN TO DELIVER ISRAEL OUT OF
   THE HAND OF THE PHILISTINES 9
   - Samson and the Philistines 9
   - The birth of the deliverer 10
   - Synopsis of Samson's life 11

2. THE CHILD SHALL BE A NAZIRITE TO GOD FROM
   THE WOMB 15
   - Samson as judge of Israel 15
   - Samson, Samuel and John the Baptist 17
   - The true Nazirite 18

3. HIS NAME IS WONDERFUL 21
   - God with us 21
   - And His name will be called Wonderful 22
   - Then He did a miracle 23

4. OUT OF THE EATER CAME SOMETHING TO EAT,
   AND OUT OF THE STRONG CAME SOMETHING
   SWEET 27
   - Stronger than the lion 27
   - Three important lessons 28
   - The secret of Christ's cross and resurrection 30

5. THE SPRING OF THE CALLER 33
   - Samson's struggle with the Philistines 33
   - Living in the rock 34
   - Water out of the rock 36

6. THE STRONG AND THE STRONGER 39
   - The strong city of Gaza 39
   - The hill that faces Hebron 41
   - The gates of Hades shall not prevail against it 41

7. PLEASE, TELL ME WHERE YOUR GREAT
   STRENGTH LIES? 43
   - Samson and Delilah 43
   - The riddle revealed 45
   - The secret of our spiritual strength 45

8. THE DYING CONQUEROR 49
   - The end of Samson's life 49
   - Samson and Christ 50

BIBLIOGRAPHY 53

INTRODUCTION

M any know Samson only as a strong man, or as a dramatic figure in his relationship with Delilah. Often these are distorted ideas about the biblical facts. That also other totally different conclusions can be drawn is unfortunately very often unknown. Samson as a type of Christ...how is that possible? Still, it is my positive conviction that this is actually the case and it is then also my intention in these Bible studies on Judges 13-16 to focus all attention on Him.

There is a clear line in Scripture that runs from Samson to David and then on to Christ as the great Redeemer of His people. And behind the Philistines, Samson's arch-enemies, we perceive the power of Satan, God's great adversary – for the Philistines were idol worshippers; they worshipped demonic powers. Just as Samson broke their neck, so to speak (Judg. 15:8), so Christ has triumphed over His powerful enemy – already during His life, but even more so on the cross of Golgotha.

Next to these important prophetic lessons from the life of Samson, we also hope to draw practical lessons for our own lives as Christians. For just as Samson was a *Nazirite* from his birth – someone who was especially consecrated for the Lord's service, so our lives as Christians are also to be fully consecrated to God. As New Testament believers, we also have been given "a spirit (or, Spirit) of power" (2 Tim. 1:7), not in order to do all kinds of power tricks, signs and wonders, but through the power of the Spirit to live and walk as renewed, spiritual people for the glory of God. In this respect, Samson is also a warning to us, for the strong hero who conquered the lion and carried away the city gates of Gaza on his shoulders could not control his own spirit. He did indeed break the ropes of his enemies, but not the shackles of his own lusts.

There are, next to the breaking of the bonds of the men of Judah (15:14) and those of Delilah (16:4 and following), seven other heroic acts to be seen in the life of Samson and it is perhaps good to name them as an introduction:

(1) The defeat of the roaring lion (14:5 and following).

(2) The defeat of thirty Philistines in Ashkelon (14:19).

(3) The destruction of the Philistines' harvest (15:3-5).

(4) The heavy blow he gave the Philistines, because they had burnt his wife and her father with fire (15:7-8).

(5) The slaying of a thousand men with a donkey's jawbone at Lehi (15:14-16).

(6) The carrying away of the city gate of Gaza (16:3).

(7) The slaying of approximately three thousand men and women at his death (16:23 and following).

May the example of Samson inspire us in the conflict with the enemy, to be "strengthened with all might, according to His glorious power, for all patience and longsuffering with joy" (Col. 1:11).

London, Spring 2001

1

HE SHALL BEGIN TO DELIVER ISRAEL
OUT OF THE HAND OF
THE PHILISTINES

*This first chapter forms a short introduction to the life
and service of Samson. Judges 13 to 16 clearly present the great
conflict with the Philistines. From Samson a line runs to David
and finally to Christ, the true Saviour of His people.*

Judges 13:5

Samson and the Philistines

At the announcement of the miraculous birth of Samson, the
Angel of the Lord said to the wife of Manoah (her name is not
given) that the son that she would bear, *should begin* to deliver
Israel out of the hand of the Philistines. It is striking to see how
exact God's Word is, even in the smallest detail. First of all, we
see here that *the Philistines* were the greatest enemy of the
Israelites in those days; they formed, in fact, an occupying
power (10:17; 14:4 and 15:11). The remark at the end of Judges
15 is also significant, where it is recorded that Samson judged
Israel for twenty years *in the days of the Philistines* (15:20). One
after the other, Samuel, Saul and David would also have to take
on this formidable adversary, as we see in 1 and 2 Samuel.

Secondly, it stands out that Samson should only *begin* to

deliver Israel out of the hand of the Philistines. The ultimate deliverance from the power of this arch-enemy was not the work of a judge but that of *King David*, the man after God's heart (2 Sam. 5:17-25; 8:1). Samson's appearance only gave a first start to Israel's deliverance. This task would eventually be completed through the victories of David who, even more so than Samson, was a type of the Messiah, the great Redeemer of God's people. For us as New Testament believers, the allusion is clear enough: the line runs from Samson to David and then on to Christ. Only *He* could truly *complete* the deliverance. In this small book we want all attention to fall on Him as the great Saviour of His people. And behind the Philistines, who served idols (demons, 1 Cor. 10:20), we perceive the power of Satan, God's great opponent. Christ has gloriously triumphed over him.

The Book of Judges further records the victory of Shamgar over the Philistines. He killed six hundred men with an ox goad (3:31). This resembles Samson's battle in Judges 15 where he used a donkey's jawbone (also a contemptuous weapon) to kill an army of one thousand men (15:15). According to 1 Samuel 13:19-22, the Philistines did not allow the Hebrews to make swords or spears. So heavy was the Philistine yoke upon them in the days of Saul and it was probably not very different in the time of Samson.

The birth of the deliverer

Another important point is that the birth, life and appearance of Samson was an act of *God's sovereign grace*. The Israelites had not *asked* for it and they had not *earned* it either. In Judges 13 we read not a single word of repentance over the evil that they had practised and so the Lord God allowed them to be handed over into the power of the Philistines, for forty years in total, until the days of Samuel (13:1; 15:20; 1 Sam. 7:2 and following). By the expression "evil in the sight of the LORD" was meant the sin of *idolatry*. The Israelites served the idols of the surrounding peoples and not the slightest effort was undertaken to turn to the living and true God. There was no joint prayer for deliverance from the power of the enemy, no humility before God – as we see on earlier occasions when the Israelites found themselves in need and called out to God (3:9,15; 4:3; 6:7; 10:10 and following).

Still, God gave a deliverer, although He allowed His people to be in the hands of the adversary for forty years (this number most often stands for a complete period of testing in the Bible). It was pure grace from God, just as the sending of His Son was an act of pure grace after all the failures of the first man. This could only flow out of God's great goodness and mercy. God cared about His people; He had pity on them and He looked after them. In Manoah and his wife we see a "believing remnant" just as there was in the time of the coming of Christ to His people (see the first chapters of the Gospel of Luke). They longed to serve the Lord and honour Him. Therefore Manoah brought a burnt offering and a grain offering and offered this to God on a rock altar (13:19-20).

Samson was born into this believing family, from parents who had enjoyed a personal encounter with the Lord God: the Angel of the Lord appeared to both of them (13:21-22). And Samson was consecrated to God from the womb, totally set apart for His service. From his birth he was a Nazirite to God (13:5). In chapter 2 we shall look at this concept of the "Nazirite" (meaning "consecrated one") more closely. Samson was the instrument that God used for the deliverance of His people. Whenever the Spirit of the Lord came upon him he was invincible – an impressive channel of divine, supernatural strength.

Synopsis of Samson's life

Judges 13 describes his birth and his youth; Judges 14 his

marriage and the riddle that led to his first confrontation with the Philistines. In Judges 15 Samson's struggle with the Philistines reached a temporary climax. He broke their might and dealt them a heavy blow after he first destroyed the harvest of the Philistines. And when the men of Judah wanted to extradite him as a prisoner, he used a jawbone to kill another thousand Philistine men. This chapter ends with the closing comment that he judged Israel for twenty years (15:20).

Chapter 16 goes on to describe Samson's fall and death. This chapter has the character of an appendix, but it also exhibits parallels with chapters 14 and 15. Twice there was a secret in Samson's life that he had to reveal at the insistence of a woman. We also find a prayer by Samson twice. Unfortunately, it went quickly downhill, however, with the judge of Israel, not only in a moral and spiritual sense but also literally (16:1,4). He ended his life in the prison of Gaza where he was forced to perform slave labour while shackled with two copper chains. After Delilah (this name means "coquettish") robbed him of his moral and spiritual strength as a Nazirite as well as the sign of his devotion to God (his long hair), he also lost his physical strength, his freedom and even his eyesight.

This sad ending was actually redeemed by the fact that God made him strong one more time. Then Samson braced himself against the two middle pillars which supported the temple of Dagon so that the building collapsed on top of those present (approximately three thousand men and women). So the dead that he killed at his death were more numerous than those he had killed in his life. Moreover, he was not buried in the land of the enemy but in the family grave, the grave of his father Manoah (this name means "rest") (16:30,31).

In closing, we must point out the great difference between Samson's appearance and that of earlier judges that judged Israel. Samson, namely, stood completely alone. Just like Antipas, there was a time when he even stood against his own people (15:11-13; cf. Rev. 2:13). This was totally different from earlier histories in the Book of Judges. The judges always had fellow warriors, even if their numbers were sometimes reduced so that only God would be given the honour for the victory (cf. Judg. 7:2). Samson, however, had no helpers in his battle with the Philistines. The Israelites resigned themselves to their fate and did not rally to the side of their deliverer.

Even though Samson often had personal motives for his battle (such as retribution or revenge), God's strength in and through him was active, striking and undeniable. This made him, in the midst of the whole decline of God's people, a unique instrument of the Spirit of God. Just as Samson in the end was shackled and handed over to the occupying Philistines by his own people, in the same way the Lord Jesus was shackled by men of His own race and handed over to the occupying Romans. In this respect, Samson is a real type of the Saviour who, abandoned even by His disciples, also had to fight the battle all alone.

2

THE CHILD SHALL BE A NAZIRITE
TO GOD FROM THE WOMB

*In this chapter we will focus specifically on the fact that Samson
was a Nazirite, which is a strong argument for viewing him
as a type of Christ. We see his permanent devotion to God reflected
in the lives of Samuel and of John the Baptist,
but above all in that of Christ Himself.*

Judges 13:5

Samson as judge of Israel

Although Samson failed miserably in his personal life, and
thereby reflected the low moral level that characterized the
people of God in those days, he is in other respects a clear type
of the Messiah. The Epistle to the Hebrews mentions him as one
of the heroes of faith, who were valiant in battle and turned to
flight the armies of the aliens (Heb. 11:32-34). In Judges 13 we
find a number of points that confirm this parallel with our Lord
Jesus, the great Redeemer of His people.

The fact that Samson, as judge, was called to commence the
deliverance of Israel from the might of the Philistines is the first
indication for this. The heroes that time and again rescued the
people from the oppression of their enemies were forerunners
of the coming king that would free Israel once and for all from

the adversaries (think of King David). In those days there was still no king in Israel, as the closing verse of the Book of Judges emphasizes. The Israelites had to make do with the rule of the judges and their administration of justice.

Samson was judge over Israel for twenty years and he acted all alone. Nobody helped him; even his own people were against him (15:11). This forms a big contrast with the beginning period of the judges when the judges were often army commanders who let the people share in the victory. It means that the power to deliver Israel was now concentrated in one person – also in a very literal sense! That makes Samson, the twelfth and last judge that is described in the Book of Judges, likewise a type of Christ, who was also rejected by His own and who brought about the redemption of His people completely by Himself.

Samson came from the tribe of Dan, and this name means *judge*. The last words of Jacob at the end of the address to his fifth son allude to this: "Dan shall *judge* his people as one of the tribes of Israel" (Gen. 49:16; cf. 30:6). The manner with which Dan took the law into his own hands appeared, at times, to be extremely suspicious (see Judg. 18). We will let this issue rest for now. The office of judge itself was honourable and pointed ultimately to the lordship of Him who, through the prophet Micah, is named "the One to be ruler in Israel", whose goings forth have been from of old, from everlasting (Mic. 5:1-2).

The naming of Samson also points in this direction because his own name means: "as the sun", or "sun man". With his arrival, a new day broke, so to speak, for God's people. In this respect he is a type of Christ as the Sun of Righteousness (Mal. 4:2). When He appears, a new morning without clouds dawns for Israel and for the world (2 Sam. 23:3-4). Christ is the great Light that rules over the day. His reign implies divine blessing for those who fear Him, and they can now reflect His light in a dark world. Moreover, they shall share in His royal reign over the earth. The picture of the rising sun is also applicable to them, as the song of Deborah already indicates: "But let those who love Him be *like the sun when it comes out* in full strength" (5:31). The New Testament confirms this. Jesus said to His disciples: "Then the righteous will shine forth as the sun in the kingdom of their Father" (Matt. 13:43).

Samson, Samuel and John the Baptist

If we now return to Judges 13, then we still see a few other points of agreement between Samson and Christ Himself as the Saviour of His people, the true Nazirite of God. First of all, there was the peculiar birth of the deliverer. The wife of Manoah was barren until that time, but the Angel of the Lord brought her the joyful news that she would become pregnant and would bear a son. Samson's birth depended on a special intervention on God's part, like the birth of Samuel from barren Hannah, for that matter, and that of John the Baptist from barren Elizabeth.

Of course, the birth of the Lord Jesus from the virgin Mary was absolutely unique. No other human deliverer is comparable with Christ Himself, but we carefully draw a few parallels. Just as the Holy One born of Mary (Luke 1:35) was the true Nazirite, whose entire life was dedicated to God, so Samson was a "Nazirite to God" from his mother's womb until the day of his death. A Nazirite was a "consecrated one", someone who was set apart for God's service according to special regulations. But it is striking to notice in this instance that it had to do with being a *permanent* Nazirite, while the Nazirite vow of Numbers 6 was of a *temporary* nature. So, in the case of Samson, God made a claim on the *whole* life of His servant.

It is definitely not a coincidence that we also come across this permanent role as a Nazirite in the case of Samuel and of John the Baptist, both of whom were "forerunners" (of Israel's first king and of the great King Himself, respectively). The deeply sorrowful Hannah made a vow that she would give her son to the Lord all the days of his life and that no razor would come upon his head (1 Sam. 1:11). And with the announcement of the birth of John the Baptist by the Angel Gabriel, we read that the child would be filled with the Holy Spirit *even from his mother's womb* and would drink neither wine nor strong drink (Luke 1:15).

These two specific characteristics of a Nazirite are important: the wearing of long hair and the abstaining from wine and strong drink. We come across these characteristics in Samson's case, as well. Samson's long hair, a symbol of his total dependence on God (cf. 1 Cor. 11:15, Rev. 9:8), is, of course, well-known. His enormous strength was coupled to this (16:17).

But the prohibition of wine or intoxicating drink was also directed towards Manoah and his wife. It was even given extra emphasis as a direction *for the mother* of the Nazirite: "Now therefore, please be careful not to drink wine or similar drink, and not to eat any unclean thing" (13:4,7,14). The behaviour of parents is of great importance in shaping their children. It is interesting that the woman was not allowed to *eat* anything unclean. We do not find this in the instructions for the Nazirite vow in Numbers 6, where it is, in fact, emphasized that the Nazirite himself may not *touch* anything unclean (i.e. a dead body). For a warrior such as Samson, this most likely would have imposed too many restrictions.

The true Nazirite

These then are the three specific characteristics according to the Book of Numbers of a Nazirite, the believer who is consecrated to God: complete dependence on God, sobriety and watchfulness (cf. 1 Thess. 5:6ff.), and holiness and purity in an impure world. Are these things visible in our lives? It really has to do with the characteristics of Christ's own life. Do we exhibit the features of Christ, who was completely and entirely consecrated to His God and Father?

In our day and age it is perhaps more important than ever

to exhibit the character traits of a Nazirite and in this way to be a channel for God's strength.

After this we see how the Angel of the Lord, the Man of God (13:6,8), left Manoah and his wife: He ascended in the flame that went up from the altar toward heaven (13:20; cf. 6:21). God's merciful dealings with His people were always based upon the value of the sacrifice, actually even from the fall of mankind. One day the true Saviour would come and share in flesh and blood (Heb. 2:14). He would be born as a Child. As the Man of sorrows, He would offer up His life on the cross of Golgotha and afterwards, by virtue of His finished work, ascend once again into heaven. The wonderful actions of the Angel of the Lord (an intimation of Christ before the incarnation; cf. Gen. 18; Ex. 23:20-23; Judg. 2:1-5) were a foretaste of this.

The last verses of Judges 13 record briefly that Samson was born and that he grew and the Lord blessed him. Luke speaks in similar terms about how John the Baptist and Jesus grew up (Luke 1:80; 2:40). The chapter ends with the announcement that the *Spirit of the Lord* began to urge Samson on in preparation for his task as an instrument in God's hand (to move is literally "to beat", hence to impel or agitate). This reminds us of how Jesus, as the true Nazirite, was led *by the Spirit* into the wilderness (Luke 4:1). With Him we fortunately do not see any trace of the failings that were so characteristic of Samson's further life. Christ's devotion was complete, till the very end, even till death.

The Spirit of the Lord began to move upon him in Mahaneh Dan (meaning "Camp of Dan") between Zorah and Eshtaol (13:25). Mahaneh Dan was the army camp of the Danites who emigrated to the north (18:2, 11-12). Samson began his task in his own surroundings. The disciples had to do the same as they testified of their Lord in their own surroundings after the outpouring of the Holy Spirit. They began as *soldiers* for Christ in Jerusalem. This principle holds true for us as well.

3

HIS NAME IS WONDERFUL

Samson's birth was a miracle, but that was even more the case with the birth of Christ from the Virgin Mary. His Name really is Wonderful, for after the wonder of the incarnation came His wondrous death, resurrection and ascension.

Judges 13:17-18

God with us

When Jacob, during his struggle by the ford of Jabbok, asked the name of the Man with whom he was wrestling, initially he received the same answer as Manoah did: "Why is it that you ask about My name?" (Gen. 32:29). The question was therefore answered with a counter-question. Of course it is good that a person asks of God, that he inquires about the Name which is above every name. But does he then actually know *what* he wants to know? That friendly question is necessary for small human beings. Do we truly realize with Whom we are dealing? Can our motives for learning to know God endure the critical test?

The name of the Man with whom Jacob wrestled, the name of the Angel of the Lord that appeared to Manoah: it was, of course, only completely revealed in New Testament times. Now we know this wonderful name and can openly express it: it is the name of Jesus, who wanted to save His people from their sins (Matt. 1:21). This name remained hidden in the Old Testament. The time was not yet ripe for it in Genesis, nor in Judges. Nevertheless, the answer that Manoah received went a step further than the revelation to Jacob, for the Angel of the Lord added the following words to His response: "...seeing it is wonderful" (13:18).

The Old Testament increasingly revealed more aspects of the glory of Christ until the fullness of time dawned and the miracle of the incarnation took place, through which God as Man came into the world. Isaiah prophesied about it: "For unto us a Child is born, unto us a Son is given" (Isa. 9:6). He was the true Nazirite, the true Redeemer. Samson was but a weak type of Him and the miraculous birth of this judge of Israel was only a pale shadow of the birth of the Messiah. Isaiah also prophesied about the miraculous birth of the Son of God: "Behold, the virgin shall conceive and bear a Son, and shall call His name Immanuel" (Isa. 7:14). Immanuel means: *God with us.* Compare this to what the New Testament says: God was manifested in the flesh, the Word became flesh (1 Tim. 3:16; John 1:14).

And His name will be called Wonderful

In this way Manoah received a fuller answer than Jacob, and it is also important to point out that this divine revelation and response was a result of Manoah's *prayer* (13:8-9). God reveals Himself to us when we long to come to know Him better, when we are truly prepared to listen to His voice. The reason the Angel was not able to reveal His name was because it was *wonderful.* He could not say more at that moment because the right moment in the history of salvation had not yet dawned. The Angel, therefore, gave away little regarding the secret of His Person. His name was wonderful. Manoah and his wife had to be satisfied with that.

The Angel of the Lord revealed something of His name and at the same time He hid the true essence of it. His name could not yet be declared: "...seeing it is wonderful". These words of the Angel may, nevertheless, also be understood very literally and very personally. His name truly is *Wonderful*. In fact this is one of the names of the Messiah, according to the prophet Isaiah, and even the first in a sequence of five names: "...and His name will be called *Wonderful*, Counsellor, Mighty God, Everlasting Father, Prince of Peace" (Isa. 9:6). Compare this to the miraculous birth of Isaac, the son of God's promise, from barren Sarah. Nothing is too hard or too wonderful for the Lord (Gen. 18:14 NASB note).

The significant answer of the Angel of the Lord to Manoah applies in a certain sense even to us as New Testament believers. There are so many facets to the Name that is above all names that He is also unfathomable for us. It contains so much splendour that the Lord Himself said: "No one knows the Son except the Father" (Matt. 11:27). Our reaction to God's wonderful revelation to us must, in any case, be characterized by worship and reverent wonder – just as was the case with Manoah and his wife. We should honour Him, kneel before Him and pay Him tribute, bring Him our sacrifice of praise. That is what the revelation of the Name of the Lord always brings about.

Then He did a miracle

But there is still more that demands our attention in these verses (13:19-20). The name of the Angel *was* not only wonderful, He also *did* a wonder by ascending up toward heaven in the flame of the altar. "He did a *wondrous* thing", verse 19 says. The miracle of the incarnation was followed by the miracle of Christ's death and resurrection and of His ascension.

Manoah took a young goat and a grain offering and offered this upon a rock to the Lord. The grain offering consisted of fine flour, mixed and anointed with oil. This is a type of Christ's pure human nature. He was born of the Holy Spirit and at the same time anointed with the Spirit. On the other hand, the burnt offering was a sacrifice, a bloody sacrifice, and this spoke of His being handed over to death to the glory of God the Father. Both sacrifices were a sweet savour to God. Paul alludes to this as follows: "Christ also has loved us and given Himself for us, an offering (like a grain offering) and a (bloody) sacrifice to God for a sweet-smelling aroma" (Eph. 5:2).

Notice that Manoah sacrificed a *young goat*, which was mostly a sin offering in the Old Testament – at least in the case of the collective sacrifices (see Lev. 16). For personal sacrifices, a burnt offering of a sheep or of a goat was very common indeed (see Lev. 1:10-13). Manoah's young goat was, therefore, offered to God as a burnt offering (13:16; cf. 6:19-21). A grain offering was indissolubly coupled with the burnt offering. This tells us the following: Christ's surrender unto death was, therefore, precisely of such great value because He was the pure and holy, perfect Man who had glorified God during His life on earth. He was in all respects the true Sacrifice. Sacrifices and offerings, burnt offerings and sin offerings could not please God, but only the sacrifice of the body of Christ (Heb. 10:5-10).

And after He offered Himself spotless to God, He went to heaven *by virtue of this sacrifice*. Just as the Angel Himself ascended in the flame of the altar, Jesus has seated Himself at the right hand of the Majesty in the heavens! We now understand something of His wonderful way of acting. It is the same unique Person who gave Himself as a sacrifice who is now ascended on high. It is, of course, also correct that He was taken up into glory by God, but the emphasis here lies on His own ascension. Christ has, as a Man, returned to heaven from where He came down. This is indeed marvellous in our eyes (cf. Ps. 118:22-23).

Here we can merely take the place of an onlooker, just like Manoah and his wife (and Gideon in Judg. 6). But we cannot remain unmoved, just as they could not: we shall kneel before

Him in worship and pay Him tribute from our hearts. Manoah himself did not understand very much of God's gracious purposes, as is obvious from the continuation of this story. His wife possessed more spiritual insight (13:22-23). But how is it with us? Do we take the place of worshippers with insight, when we see all the miracles of the work and of the Person of Christ? Can we say with Jacob: "I have seen God face to face, and my life is preserved" (Gen. 32:30)?

Thy name we bless, Lord Jesus,
That name all names excelling;
How great Thy love all praise above
Should every tongue be telling.

4

OUT OF THE EATER CAME SOMETHING TO EAT, AND OUT OF THE STRONG CAME SOMETHING SWEET

In this chapter we will reflect upon the special results of Christ's victory over the power of the Evil One, who continues to walk about this world as a roaring lion seeking whom he may devour.

Judges 14:14

Stronger than the lion

The story of Samson's marriage and riddle teaches us something about the blessed results of Christ's victory over the power of the adversary, who, according to Peter, "walks about like a roaring lion, seeking whom he may devour" (1 Pet. 5:8). The slain, dead lion is a picture of the devil, who met his superior in Christ. The devil is an "eater", constantly in search of prey. He is also the "strong", who guards his domain and who can only be conquered by "a stronger than he", Someone with divine power (cf. Matt. 12:29; Luke 11:21-22; Heb. 2:14-15).

Samson used these two designations in his riddle, speaking of the lion he had killed in the vineyards of Timnah (a city in the original region of the tribe of Dan at the border of Judah, where obviously Philistines also lived). The spiritual significance of

Samson's words is not difficult to understand. Christ is the stronger One who not only bound the strong eater, but also gave him the final blow, the stab of death.

Actually this last expression is not entirely correct. Samson was not carrying a weapon with him to kill the lion with. (David presumably did have one when he was tending his father's sheep and killed both lion and bear, 1 Sam. 17:34-35.) Samson gained the victory with his bare hands. The Spirit of the Lord came upon him, enabling him with his own hands to rend the lion that came roaring at him, as one would have torn apart a young goat (14:5-6). So it is, too, with the victory that Christ gained over Satan. Christ approached him in the power and worthiness that He personally possessed, without further human means. He fought the fight entirely alone and no man stood at His side. Still He gained (also through the power of God's Spirit) a sudden and definite victory over the wicked one, whose might was now broken for ever.

Three important lessons

I believe this to be the principal typological lesson of this section and we need to first let this lesson sink in thoroughly. Naturally, questions will then arise, for Satan is still the prince of this world and still walks about as a roaring lion; but these questions are of secondary importance. We must first become impressed with the tremendous and definite victory that Christ gained over His adversary. It seems that Scripture wants to teach us here:

(1) the essence of the conflict,
(2) the definite end of it, and
(3) the blessed results Christ's victory has had for His own.

(1) Christ was the Judge, the Saviour and Redeemer of His people, the Nazirite who was entirely consecrated to God from His mother's womb. He came to stand face to face with the

violent adversary who sought His life. This began as early as the temptation in the wilderness, when the devil tried to tempt Him but eventually had to depart from Him. Christ gained the victory entirely alone, because He fought in the strength of God. He did not possess any human weapon. His only weapon was the "sword" of God's Word.

(2) Then followed the years of the Lord's servant work in which He, through His might, again and again bound the "strong man" (i.e. Satan) and plundered his goods. This aspect is not at all considered here in the history of Samson. Here we find, as mentioned, only the definite result of the confrontation between the Lord and the enemy of souls. Christ gained the total victory over His adversary on Calvary's cross. As the Epistle to the Hebrews so strikingly puts it: Christ became Man, taking part in blood and flesh so that "through death He might destroy him who had the power of death, that is, the devil, and release those who through fear of death were all their lifetime subject to bondage" (Heb. 2:14-15).

Here, too, He did not use a human weapon. He conquered His adversary "through death", namely, by penetrating into the last bulwark of the enemy to rob him of his power – just as David once killed Goliath with his own sword. This victory is definite and absolute, as so many places in the New Testament assure us (John 12:31; 14:30; 16:11; Col. 2:14-15).

(3) Now, however, this victory has blessed results only *for those who believe*. This means that there is a great deal of tension; for although Satan is a conquered enemy on the one hand, on the other hand he is still walking about, seeking whom he might devour. His defeat is a settled fact but the execution of the judgment awaits the beginning of the Millennium. At its beginning, he will be bound and cast into the abyss and at the end of the thousand years he will be cast into the lake of fire and sulphur (Rev. 20:2,10).

Therefore, the food coming forth out of the eater and the

sweetness coming forth out of the strong one is not yet available to everyone. The whole creation does not yet share in the glorious results of the triumph Christ gained on the cross. That will only take place at His return. Yet in the meantime, those who are united to Him do indeed share the sweet and blessed results of His work. They taste, so to speak, of the "honey" that comes forth from the strong one – just like Samson himself ate while he went along and also gave to his father and mother of the honey out of the dead lion's carcass (14:9).

Only the "family" of the Conqueror shares in the victory at this time. Those of us who know Him and belong to Him, who hear the Word of God and do it, are His relatives, His mother and His brothers (Luke 8:21). Initially, this "family" consisted only of believers from Israel, but believers from all nations were later added.

The secret of Christ's cross and resurrection

Christ's triumph at Golgotha remains a great secret for most people, as we clearly see in this story. Even Samson's parents, his next of kin, did not know the origin of the honey their son gave them to eat. So, also, the good news of the gospel remains a mystery for the Jewish nation at this time because there lies a veil over their hearts (Rom. 11:8; 2 Cor. 3:15). And for the "Philistines", those who are professors in name only (but in fact worldly people), it is a complete mystery.

The message of the cross is even "foolishness" to those who are perishing (1 Cor. 1:18). They do not understand anything at all of the fact that salvation is to be found only in Christ, crucified; that He, through His sufferings, His atoning death and His glorious resurrection from among the dead, has annihilated all hostile powers for good; that His own people share in the sweet fruits of His work. All these things are a matter of faith: faith in God's Word, in the finished work of Christ, in God who raised Him from the dead. Without faith, it all remains a mystery, a secret, a riddle that no one can solve, not in three days, nor even in seven days (14:14-15).

Only via a roundabout way were the Philistines, the enemies of God's people, able to obtain the solution to the riddle. They pressed Samson's wife to explain it to them, but this also meant the end of the feast and heralded their own demise. It is entirely different with us who believe. God's secrets do not remain a mystery for us. The Holy Spirit Himself, who indwells us, reveals them to us, initiating us into the mysteries of God's wisdom (1 Cor. 2:6ff.).

Because of this we can repeat what the Victor says (in type): "What is sweeter than honey, what is stronger than a lion?" In other words: Nothing is to be compared to the sweet and glorious results of the work of Him who has slain the strong enemy. Christ has annulled him who had the power over death. Now we are redeemed and free. We enjoy the sweet food of peace with God, liberty from sin and death and eternal life.

Honey was one of the blessings of the promised land (Deut. 8:7-9). The land of Canaan is a picture of the heavenly places with their wealth of blessing for the Christian (Eph. 1:3). Christ's victory on the cross of shame places all of heaven's blessings in our possession. The "honey" lights up our eyes, our heart, our understanding (just as once happened with Jonathan, cf. 1 Sam. 14:27), until we appear with Christ in glory and the secret of His victory is unveiled before the eyes of all!

He Satan's power laid low;
Made sin, He sin o'erthrew;
Bowed to the grave, destroyed it so,
And death by dying slew.

5

THE SPRING OF THE CALLER

*Samson appeared to be unconquerable in his confrontations
with the enemy. Still, he turned out to be only a limited
human being, who was totally dependent upon God's help.
The Spring of the caller marked this important moment in his life.*

Judges 15:19

Samson's struggle with the Philistines

In this chapter we see how Samson's struggle with the
Philistines reached a climax and how he in this way made his
appearance as the great conqueror. It was not actually his own
victory, his own success, but the work of the Lord. Samson also
had to learn to give Him all honour for the deliverance that He
had brought about. He was merely a dependent human being,
who was the instrument in God's hand in order to bring about
this victory over the Philistines: "Then he became very thirsty;
so he cried out to the LORD and said, 'You have given this great
deliverance by the hand of Your servant; and now shall I die of
thirst and fall into the hand of the uncircumcised?' " (15:18).

At the end of Judges 14 it is evident that Samson's proposed
marriage to a Philistine led to the first confrontation with the
occupier (cf. 14:4). The wrath of the groom was aroused due to

the fact that his companions had wormed the solution to his riddle out of his Philistine bride on the seventh day of the banquet. If they had not plowed with his heifer, they would not have solved his riddle. Samson now had to make good on his promise by giving his companions thirty linen garments and thirty changes of clothing (14:12). He did this by killing thirty men in Ashkelon and gave their clothes to those who had solved the riddle. Samson returned in anger to his father's house and his wife – without him being aware of it – was given to his companion, the friend of the groom.

After a while, so Judges 15 begins, Samson went back to Timnah in the time of the wheat harvest (in 15:5 the author will return to this). He wanted to make things right again with his wife and took a gift of a young goat along with him (cf. Gen. 38:17,20,23). But, of course, the father of the woman could not act as if nothing had happened. He did not give Samson permission to go inside. This produced a new conflict with the Philistines.

Samson went and caught three hundred foxes (according to some, jackals were meant), tied them together by their tails and fastened a torch between each pair of tails. Then he set the torches on fire and drove the animals into the standing grain of the Philistines. All of the standing grain as well as the olive groves were destroyed. In revenge, the Philistines burned the former wife of Samson and her father with fire (15:1-6). This led again to a new solo action on the part of Samson. He took revenge on them and attacked his enemies "hip and thigh with a great slaughter" (15:7-8).

Living in the rock

Then he retreated in the cleft of the rock of Etam (in Judah, east of Zorah), where he thought he would be safe for the time being. But the Philistines were out for revenge and rose up in mass, encamped in Judah, and deployed themselves against

Lehi (this name means "Jaw"; cf. 15:17). The men of Judah entered into negotiations with the enemy army. This led to the result that the men of Judah themselves then went to Samson's hiding-place (three thousand men strong!), in order to bind him and hand him over to the Philistines. Samson agreed to this, but demanded from his brothers that they themselves would not kill him. So they tied him with two new ropes and brought him out of the rock cleft with them (15:9-13).

In this way Samson had to leave his safe hiding-place in the cleft of the rock of Etam (meaning fortress, or den of beast of prey). This dwelling-place in the rock makes us think of an event in the life of Moses. When Israel had sinned badly at Mount Horeb, Moses found a place of complete safety in the hollow of the rock, in a cleft in the stone (Ex. 33:21-22). This contains the following spiritual lesson for us: in Christ, the Rock, we are completely safe from judgment and from the power of the enemy. When we are aware of our elevated position in Christ and live accordingly, no one can bring damage on us. That is a secure fortress for us as believers who are weak in ourselves (like the rock badgers who make their homes in the crags; see Prov. 30:26).

Unfortunately, Samson was taken out of the crevice by the men of Judah, who conducted themselves as accomplices of the enemy (15:13). Of course, we as Christians can never lose our position in Christ, but the enemy tries to rob us of the practical enjoyment of it. It is deeply regrettable when he, in addition, knows how to find supporters within the people of God who are also ready to hand us over to him. In such a case, we can think of deceivers such as the Judaizers who attempted to rob the Galatians of their freedom in Christ, or the false teachers who drew the Colossians away from Christ. Let us not, as Samson, allow ourselves to be tied with "two new ropes".

As soon as Samson came to Lehi and the Philistines came shouting against him, the Spirit of the Lord came mightily upon him. His bonds melted away: the ropes that were on his arms became like flax that is burned with fire (15:14). This is undoubtedly a foreboding of what would yet happen in the future. Delilah would also bind Samson with new ropes, but he would, just as now, break them off his arms like a thread (16:12). For the time being, he was unassailable to the power of the enemy. He found a fresh (and therefore strong) jawbone of a donkey and killed a thousand men with it, a large multitude of Philistines. In a four-line song he sang of his own victory:

> *"With the jawbone of a donkey,*
> *Heaps upon heaps,*
> *With the jawbone of a donkey*
> *I have slain a thousand men!"*

When Samson had finished speaking, he threw the jawbone away and called that place "Ramath Lehi", literally "Jawbone Height" (15:15-17). But was it such an honourable victory? A donkey's jawbone was a despicable weapon. Moreover, he became unclean through this: an Israelite was not allowed to touch the carcass of an unclean animal (Lev. 5:2). Worse yet was the fact that he did not give God the honour for the great victory that he had won. But wasn't he only a *servant*, an instrument in God's hand?

Water out of the rock

Because Samson forgot his smallness, God *made* him small. Suddenly he became very thirsty and was in danger of collapsing. Then all at once he again realized how totally dependent he was on his God and that he had to give Him the honour. He cried out to the Lord and said, "You have given this great deliverance by the hand of Your servant; and now shall I die of thirst and fall into the hand of the uncircumcised?" (15:18).

This *great divine deliverance* reminds us as Christians of *"so great a salvation"*, the salvation now brought about through our great Conqueror, the Lord Jesus Christ (cf. Heb. 2:3). A parallel can be found in the history of Israel in 2 Samuel 23. Shammah, one of David's mighty men, killed the Philistines at Lehi – the same place where Samson had fought. The Lord granted "a great victory" then as well (2 Sam. 23:12).

And the Lord responded to Samson's cry. His prayer was answered in a wonderful way, just as happened with his last prayer right before his death (16:28). The Lord split the rock before his eyes and water streamed from the hollow place in Lehi so that he could drink, and his vitality returned. So he revived and he called the spring: Spring of the caller. It is located at Lehi to this day, according to the author (15:19). It provided lasting refreshment.

Once again we find here the motif already mentioned from the wilderness journey of the children of Israel: the split rock of Lehi reminds us of the rock in Horeb (Ex. 17:6). The Israelites did not thirst when God led them through the wilderness. "He caused the waters to flow from the rock for them; He also split the rock, and the waters gushed out" (Isa. 48:21). This took place only after Moses struck the rock with his rod. "That Rock was Christ", Paul says emphatically (1 Cor. 10:4).

The fresh streams of water are a picture of the Holy Spirit of whom we have been made to drink (1 Cor. 12:13). It would serve us well to bear in mind that those streams flowed out of the stricken Rock. The Spirit could only be given to us after Jesus was glorified (John 7:37-39). The finished work of Christ on Calvary's cross, where He was bruised for our iniquities, was the basis for the outpouring of the Holy Spirit. It is this Spirit that makes alive and gives us new strength. It is also through the Spirit that we have access to the Father – with our prayers as well as with our praises. Do we know this Spring, the Spring of the caller? Do we belong to His priests, who call on His name?

6

THE STRONG AND THE STRONGER

*The event that comes up for discussion in this chapter has
presumably taken place at the end of Samson's career. It is obvious
that he derailed in his personal life. Yet God was still with him
so that he won an impressive victory over the enemy. The gateposts
of Gaza could not hold back Samson when he arose in the middle of
the night. Likewise, the gates of death had to yield to the power of
Christ when He awoke from His death sleep. The grave could not
hold great David's greater Son – He overcame, the conquering Hero.
That is the typological lesson from this section.*

Judges 16:3

The strong city of Gaza

The he short history at the beginning of Judges 16 contains a
beautiful type of Christ's victory over His adversary, the devil,
who had the power of death (Heb. 2:14). The verse to which I
want to draw attention in this connection is as follows: "He
arose at midnight, took hold of the doors of the gate of the city
and the two gateposts, pulled them up, bar and all, put them on
his shoulders, and carried them to the top of the hill that faces
Hebron" (16:3).

We will once again pass by the tragic failings of Samson as a Nazirite and as the judge of Israel and will concentrate on our subject: Samson as a type of *Christ*. It is really the same lesson which we found in the story of the slain and dead lion, but the emphasis is different. The story of Judges 14 was about the personal conflict with the enemy, the "man-to-man" struggle and the complete victory won by the Nazirite of God.

In Judges 16 the subject is not a personal conflict, but the victory over *a city*. This city and its gates symbolize the power the enemy exercises over all those who find themselves in his domain. It is this collective aspect which we hope to develop still further. It concerned naturally a *Philistine* city, since that was the enemy that Samson contended with during his entire life. He judged Israel "twenty years in the days of the Philistines" (15:20), in the years in which the Philistines ruled over the Israelites (cf. 15:11).

The incident with which chapter 16 begins, has presumably taken place at the end of his career. Samson went to Gaza. He went, so to speak, to the lion's den, and his enemies thought they could kill him there. Gaza was the most prominent of the five Philistine royal cities. Gaza meant "the strong". The closing scene of his life, this chapter ends with (16:21), would also take place in this capital city of the Philistines.

In this strong city we have a picture of the power of the devil, who had dominion over the dead. The devil tried to hold Christ captive when He died and penetrated into the last stronghold of the enemy. The crucified and dead Christ has, however, won a great victory. The "strong city" of the enemy is now abased, its fortress lies open and its power is destroyed (cf. Isa. 25:2). To use the words of Paul: it is true that Christ has descended into the lower parts of the earth when He was laid in the dust of death. But now Christ is risen from the dead. The One who descended is also the One who ascended. And ascended on high, He has "led captivity captive" (Eph. 4:8).

The hill that faces Hebron

His triumph is complete – just like that of Samson, who arose at midnight and took hold of the doors of the gate of the city and pulled them up with gateposts and bars and all (16:3). The locked gate could not hold back Samson – just as death could not hold on to Christ. He broke even the cords of death. His name is: Lord of life. When He arose from the dead, He won a glorious victory over death and the grave by leaving these things permanently behind Him. He is risen and He is also the One who ascended on high. That is even higher than Samson who climbed with his trophy to the top of the hill that faces Hebron.

Hebron was the place where the patriarchs lived and where they were buried also. It was the place of the *covenant* and the place of *communion* with God (that is the meaning of the name Hebron). This reminds us, therefore, of God's constant faithfulness to His people. He never leaves us alone, not even in the time of deepest ruin – and the end of the Book of Judges testifies all too clearly to this. From Hebron the people were always reminded by the sign of Samson's powerful victory: in the distance lay the top of the hill where Samson had carried away the gates of Gaza.

Likewise, we can now see with the eyes of faith the triumph that Christ has won (for we walk by faith, not by sight, 2 Cor. 5:7). In the joy of our communion with God and in the consciousness of His eternal faithfulness, we see the marvellous results of Christ's victory. Therefore we can speak of His heroic deeds and the sign of victory that He has seized, for He has overpowered the gates of death and hell.

The gates of Hades shall not prevail against it

Actually, there is an important collective and common aspect here as well, that we would now like to emphasize. It is not only about the personal salvation of the sinner and the personal security of the believer, though these things are also important. But the Scriptures also teach us that *the whole Church* is built on Christ, the Rock, the Son of the living God. And since He is the cornerstone and the foundation of the Church, "the gates of Hades shall not prevail against it" (Matt. 16:16-18).

The *gates* symbolize the power and authority of the enemy. But Easter has come: Christ is risen. Now no power of death or the grave, of sin or of Satan can defeat God's people. Captivity is led captive. The doors of the last fortress of the enemy stand open and his prisoners have been set free. The bronze gates are broken, the iron bars are cut in two, the psalmist says. Therefore, we can praise the Lord for His goodness and for His wonderful works to the children of men (Ps. 107:15-16). Can you join in with this song of praise?

> *Risen Christ, our souls adore Thee:*
> *Thou hast left the silent grave;*
> *Death and Hades quail before Thee,*
> *Thou art mighty now to save:*
> *Glory, glory, we adore Thee,*
> *And the Victor's banner wave.*

> *Risen Lord, Thou now art seated*
> *On the Father's throne on high;*
> *God the place supreme has meted*
> *To the One who came to die:*
> *All completed, Hell defeated,*
> *Glory, glory, Lord, we cry.*

7

PLEASE, TELL ME WHERE YOUR GREAT STRENGTH LIES?

In this chapter the secret of Samson's mighty strength finally comes to light. The great riddle is solved by Delilah's craftiness, but it leads to Samson's demise. When his strength leaves him, he becomes an easy prey for the Philistines. In this connection, however, we also want to reflect upon our own spiritual strength as believers.

Judges 16:6

Samson and Delilah

What was the secret of Samson's amazing strength? In this chapter his special strength appears to be connected to his being a Nazirite and to his long hair as a distinguishing feature of his devotion to God (16:17). The story reaches a critical point here since Samson gives away the riddle of his life, which had always been well-guarded until then, to Delilah. She was the third Philistine woman who played a role in his life, even though such an unequal yoke was clearly forbidden by the LORD (Deut. 7:2-4). She lived in the Valley of Sorek (which means "grapevine"); this name points out the fertility of the valley. In the same valley also lay the vineyards of Timnah and the places of Zorah and Eshtaol. Possibly Samson regularly visited Delilah in the Valley of Sorek from his own home in or near Zorah. Here it is not the case of a legal marriage as in chapter 14, even though Delilah is not called a harlot as is the woman whom Samson visited in Gaza (16:1).

A believer cannot sin in a cheap or easy way. Sin is never cheap for a believer. If we do not flee the sin of sexual immorality, it will overpower us (Gen. 39:7ff.; 1 Cor. 6:18).

It was quickly noticed that Samson had developed a love for Delilah and the lords of the Philistines tried to avail themselves of the opportunity. Delilah had to find out where Samson got this great strength and by what means he could be overpowered. The five lords would each give her eleven hundred pieces of silver, undoubtedly a royal reward (16:4-5). But it actually turned out to be no easy task to discover the great riddle of Samson's life. Delilah needed all her seductive charms in order to worm the secret of his extraordinary strength out of him.

Samson misled her three times. The first two times are parallel: first he allowed himself to be tied with seven (the number of completeness!) fresh bowstrings, then with new ropes that had never been used (cf. 15:13). But each time he easily broke the strong bonds as soon as Delilah called to him, "The Philistines are upon you, Samson!" We also read in this account the significant words, "So the secret of his strength was not known" (16:9).

The third time actually became risky because Delilah continued to press him and so Samson gave in and mentioned his hair. In this symbol of his Nazirite vow, that spoke of complete submission and consecration, lay the secret of his strength. He did not tell Delilah the whole truth: if she wove the seven (!) locks of his head into the web of the loom, then he would not be able to come loose. But when he awoke from his sleep he pulled out the batten and the web from the loom (16:13-14).

The riddle revealed

The next verses show many similarities with chapter 14. Samson's bride at that time also pressed him and kept on questioning him until he told her the solution to the riddle. Her reproach that Samson did not really love her was repeated by Delilah almost word-for-word. Eventually the strong hero succumbed. He became vexed to death and told her all his heart: "No razor has ever come upon my head, for I have been a Nazirite to God from my mother's womb. If I am shaven, then my strength will leave me, and I shall become weak, and be like any other man" (16:17).

Delilah grabbed her chance with both hands and took the necessary measures. When she had the seven locks of his head shaved off, his strength also left him. It was in actuality the Lord Himself that left him, but Samson only realized this after it was too late (16:19-20). He now formed an easy prey for the Philistines, who put out the eyes of their prisoner, took him away and bound him with bronze fetters (the same thing happened to King Zedekiah during the downfall of the kingdom of the two tribes, 2 Kings 25:7). In the prison in Gaza he was made to turn the mill that ground the grain (16:21).

Was this now the fameless end of the judge of Israel? No, thankfully not. God did not abandon Samson, not even in the prison where he had to spend his days as a slave. This part of the story ends with the promising words, "However, the hair of his head began to grow again after it had been shaven" (16:22). That gave hope for the future, because God would make him strong one more time and give him a glorious victory over the Philistines. But that is the topic of our next chapter.

The secret of our spiritual strength

We now want to take a moment to look at the meaning of this story in the light of the New Testament. What is the secret of *our* spiritual strength and how do we handle it? We have already noticed that Samson's strength left him immediately when he lost the symbol of his dedication to God. The LORD was no longer with him after the seven locks of his head were shaved off. Samson boasted about his own strength, but that appeared to be in vain. His great strength was gone. The Spirit of the Lord, that time and again had come upon him (13:25; 14:6,19; 15:14), had now departed from him.

In this connection it is good to point out immediately an important difference with the position of the New Testament believer, who is blessed with the *permanent indwelling* of the Spirit of God (cf. John 14:15-17; Rom. 8:9-11; 1 Cor. 2:12; 2 Cor. 1:22; Eph. 1:13-14; 2 Tim. 1:14). The Spirit will not leave us, but we can hinder the workings of the Holy Spirit or even make them almost impossible. We can grieve the Holy Spirit (Eph. 4:30), or even quench the Spirit (1 Thess. 5:19) by wrong behaviour.

The great difference with the Old Testament dispensation, however, remains valid. The Spirit did not yet dwell on the earth in the Church (for it was not yet formed), nor did He indwell the individual believer. We always read that the Spirit *came upon* someone in order to equip him for a special task (cf. Judg. 3:10; 6:34; 11:29; 1 Sam. 10:6,10; 11:6; 16:13; Ps. 51:13). Only after Jesus was glorified in heaven did the Spirit come to the earth to have His dwelling place for ever in the redeemed (John 7:39, 1 Cor. 3:16; 6:19).

Let us not make light of this blessing, or play with it as Samson did with being a Nazirite. Let us not pride ourselves on it either, as Samson did in his presumption. He trusted in his own strength: " 'I will go out as before, at other times, and shake myself free!' But he did not know that the LORD had departed from him" (16:20). In the New Testament we find in this respect a striking parallel with the words of those in Laodicea, who also boasted about their supposed privileges, but did not realize that they were in fact wretched, miserable, poor, blind and naked (Rev. 3:17). Samson was also spiritually blind, for he did not realize his actual condition (that he was totally powerless now that the LORD had left him), and after this followed his literal blindness when the Philistines took him and put out his eyes (16:21). And a wretched and pitiful lot awaited him in the prison in Gaza.

The important lesson from this section is that we must not speak in a wrong way about our special privileges and blessings. We must not betray the secret of our spiritual strength to people with bad motives, "Philistines", nominal Christians who want to rob us of our strength and our freedom and bring us into captivity. This was, for example, what happened with the foolish Galatians (Gal. 2:4). They were bewitched by false teachers (Gal. 3:1), just as Samson allowed himself to be bewitched by Delilah. This eventually led to spiritual blindness and slavery (Gal. 4:9; 5:1), just as it did with Samson in the literal sense of the word. Let us therefore conduct ourselves as true Nazirites and not abandon the secret of our consecration, that is, the anointing of the Spirit and our total dependence on God. May the Lord grant that our thoughts would not be drawn away from the simple and pure consecration to Christ by the seductive charms of the enemy.

8

THE DYING CONQUEROR

The life of Samson did not have a happy ending. It was sad and tragic, but actually in his death he won his greatest victory. This is a picture of the work of Christ, who in His death redeemed us and because of the cross gained the greatest triumph over the powers of Satan, sin and death.

Judges 16:30

The end of Samson's life

The end of Samson's life is a striking type of Christ's last and final victory over the power of the enemy. *In his death* lay his greatest victory, for we read here that he killed more enemies in his death than in his life. "Then Samson said, 'Let me die with the Philistines!' And he pushed with all his might, and the temple fell on the lords and all the people who were in it. So the dead that he killed at his death were more than he had killed in his life" (16:30). But this principle is even more applicable to the Lord Jesus, who by the death of the cross gained His greatest triumph over the powers of Satan, sin and death. He descended into the grave, but He was also raised from the dead. He is the Resurrection and the Life, the One who was dead and is alive for evermore. He has the keys of Hades and of Death (Rev. 1:17-18).

In the light of these great things, the Old Testament type turns pale. It is fading in comparison to the full New Testament reality. Samson died *with* his enemies, but Christ died *for* His enemies. Samson wanted to take *revenge* on the Philistines and in this way to perish with them, but Christ died *out of love* for the lost. Samson was buried in the grave of his father Manoah, and that was the definite end of his career. But Christ is risen from the grave and we, His former enemies, are also risen *with Him* to a new life. Approximately three thousand Philistines were killed when Samson died (16:27), but when the Church was born on the day of Pentecost, approximately three thousand souls were saved (Acts 2:41).

For the Church there is nothing more important than to remember the death of our Lord and to proclaim it again and again at His Table (cf. 1 Cor. 10 and 11). The Lord's death, the death of Him who is Lord of all, is a miracle that we will never be able to fathom, but it brings us time and again to real praise and worship. So we proclaim His death – the first Church did that *daily* – until He returns, for the crucified Conqueror is alive for evermore and He is coming quickly! And we marvel continually at the great secret of His death, as we died with Him and were raised with Him too.

Samson and Christ

On the other hand there is, of course, a very significant *moral* difference between Samson and Christ. The type turns out to be in many respects an *anti*type, just as is the case with so many Old Testament examples – to begin with Adam (cf. Rom. 5:14ff.). The failures of the first man bring to light the perfections of the *second* Man, the Lord from heaven.

This is evident in more respects in this case. The true Nazirite has never given away the secret of His consecration to God. He was faithful unto death. He only did the will of His heavenly Father and did not deviate for one minute from the path that His God and Father had laid out for Him.

Samson, however, succumbed repeatedly to temptations. Twice he gave away his secret under pressure from a woman: in chapter 14 to the Philistine from Timnah and in chapter 16 to Delilah. The strong hero that could capture a city could not rule his spirit (Prov. 16:32).

Christ went up to Jerusalem to voluntarily give Himself there as a sacrifice. With Samson, on the other hand, we see a descending line, literally and also figuratively. It was a path that went downhill, actually, even from the beginning of his career when he went down to Timnah (14:1). Here he went down to the Valley of Sorek and once again entered into a relationship with a Philistine woman (16:4). This was not a legal marriage as was the case in chapter 14. Delilah let him fall asleep on her knees, and called for a man and had him shave off the seven locks of his head. So he was robbed of his mighty strength, but even more so deprived of his freedom and his eyesight. The Philistines carried him away to Gaza and threw him into prison. There he had to turn the mill that ground the grain like a slave.

The only sign of hope in this pitiful tale forms the marginal note: "However, the hair of his head began to grow again after it had been shaven" (16:22). Samson's unusual strength was connected to this outward sign of his complete consecration to God, yes, the presence of the LORD Himself was coupled with this. By the way, this is not valid for the New Testament believer, because he enjoys the *permanent indwelling* of the Holy Spirit – although it remains true that our inner devotedness determines our outward behaviour and our outward strength (see chapter 7 on this subject).

So Samson was gradually made ready for the *last* confrontation with his enemies. His dependence on God grew along with his hair. In the prison he learned again how to pray. And his last wish to die with the Philistines really was fulfilled. God gave him back his supernatural strength one more time, after he was first an object of amusement for his enemies (just as Jesus was mocked before He died). Samson had to entertain them with music and song. The "show" (cf. Ex. 32:6) of Samson, who was possibly also artistically gifted, was in actuality the prelude of their own demise.

The important point here is not so much the rehabilitation of Samson himself, but the tremendous confrontation between Dagon, the god of the Philistines, and the God of Israel, the living and true God. Dagon (possibly a grain god), to whom the Philistines attributed their victory over Samson (16:23-24), therefore had to get the worst of it. When Samson braced himself with strength against the two middle pillars which supported the temple, the temple of the idol collapsed and buried the Philistines *with* their idols. This theme returns in 1 Samuel where Dagon had to bow, so to speak, before the God of Israel and pay tribute to Him. Dagon had fallen on his face to the earth before the ark of the LORD and he turned out to be totally powerless (1 Sam. 5:3-4).

Glory be to our Lord, who through His death and resurrection has triumphed over all idolatrous powers! One day every knee will bow and every tongue confess that Jesus Christ is Lord, to the glory of God the Father (Phil. 2:8-11).

BIBLIOGRAPHY

Barber, C.J., *Judges: A narrative of God's Power*, Neptune, New Jersey 1990.

Bruce, F.F., *Judges*, in 'New Bible Commentary', Leicester 1970.

Daalen, A.G. van, *Simson Verwijst*, in 'Geen koning in die dagen', Baarn 1982.

Goslinga, C.J., *Het boek der Richteren*, in 'Korte Verklaring', Kampen n.d.

Inrig, G., *Gottes Kraft reicht weiter, ein Gang durch das Buch der Richter*, Dillenburg 1982.

Keil, C.F. and Delitzsch, F., *The Book of Judges*, Grand Rapids 1980.

Kelly, W., *Lectures on the Book of Judges*, London 1945.

Oeveren, B. van, *Richteren*, in 'Tekst voor tekst', 's Gravenhage 1987.

Oosterhoff, B.J., *Het boek Richteren*, in 'Bijbel met verklarende kanttekeningen', Baarn n.d.

Rossier, H., *Opwekkingen, beschouwing over het boek Richteren*, 's Gravenhage n.d.

CHAPTER TWO PUBLICATIONS

Order Code

André, G.
123146 More Fruit, the Father's Loving Discipline, pb   £   1.25
Bouter, A.E.
113399 Behold, I Stand at the Door, pb   £   1.95
123203 Servants of God, pb   £   1.95
Bouter, H.
123018 The Ark of the Covenant, pb, 2nd edition   £   2.95
123028 Bethel, The Dwelling Place of the God of Jacob, pb,
  2nd ed.   £   2.95
123046 Christ, the Wisdom of God, pb, 2nd ed.   £   1.25
123062 Divine Design, God's Plan of Salvation, pb   £   1.25
123107 In the Beginning (Genesis 1-11), pb   £   2.95
123112 Jacob's Last Words, pb, 2nd ed.   £   2.95
123114 John, the Beloved Disciple, pb, 2nd ed.   £   1.25
123185 Reflections on the Greatness of our Lord, pb, 2nd ed.   £   1.25
190069 The Healing of Naaman, pb   £   1.25
Bull, G.T.
123194 The Rock and the Sand, Glimpses of the Life of Faith, pb £   5.95
Darby, J.N.
123170 Pilgrim Portions, pb   £   3.95
Deck, J.G.
123106 Hymns and Sacred Poems & brief biography, hb   £   3.95
Dennett, E.
123043 The Children of God, hb   £   8.95
Dronsfield, W.R.
123069 The Eternal Son of Father (2nd ed.), pb   £   1.30
123232 Unity and Authority (2nd printing), pb   £   1.30
Harris, J.L.
123015 Antinomianism & Legalism, pb   £   1.80
  (or, What is the Rule for Christian Conduct?)
Kelly, W.
123030 The Bible Treasury Magazine 1856/1920. 16 V. + Index   £ 250.00
123078 F.E. Raven Heterodox on Eternal Life, hb   £   2.95
123191 The Revelation, Greek Text & Translation, hb   £   5.95

123059	Daniel's Seventy Weeks, pb	£	1.30
123118	The Lamentations of Jeremiah, hb	£	3.95
123247	Unity and Fellowship, pb	£	1.95

Koechlin, J.

123213	The Tabernacle	£	1.95
	(pullout folder in English, French, German and Spanish)		

Lowe, W.J.

123151	A Nest in the Altar, hb	£	4.95

Mackintosh, C.H.

150094	Genesis to Deuteronomy – Notes on the Pentateuch, hb	£	19.95
150076	Mackintosh Treasury, hb	£	19.95
123021	The Assembly of God, pb	£	1.80
	(or, The All-sufficiency of the Name of Jesus)		
123130	The Lord's Coming, pb	£	1.95
123002	Unity, What is it and am I confessing it? pb	£	0.75

Mair, G.

123079	The Fisherman's Gospel Manual, pb	£	3.95

Reid, Wm (MA)

123126	Literature & Mission of Plymouth Brethren, pb	£	0.75

Rossier, H.L.

123237	What is a Meeting of the Assembly? pb (new ed.)	£	1.80

Rouw, J.

123083	Gems Tell Their Secret, pb, full colour	£	2.25
123206	Here is the Smallest Bible in the World, with NCR slide	£	1.50
123104	House of Go(l)d–Welcome, pb	£	1.95
123204	Shalom and Israel, pb. full colour	£	2.25

Smith, H.

190051	Guidance in the Day of ruin, pb	£	2.95

Seibel, A.

123057	The Church Subtly Deceived, pb	£	3.95

Snell, H.H.

123004	The Way of Faith in an Evil Time (2nd printing) pb	£	1.95

Stuart, C.E.

123177	Primitive Christianity & the Sufficiency of the Word, hb	£	8.95

Turner, W.G.

123113	John Nelson Darby, a biography, latest ed., pb	£	4.50

Wallace, F.

123263	Spiritual Songsters, biographical sketches of Hymnwriters, hb	£	9.95

Wijnholds, H.

123038	Called to Fellowship, pb	£	1.95

Available from: Chapter Two Trust,
Fountain House, 1a Conduit Road, Woolwich, London, SE18 7AJ, England
www.chaptertwo.org.uk, e-mail: chapter2uk@aol.com